DUCK EDWING'S
MADventures
of Almost
SUPERHEROES

Written and Illustrated by
Duck Edwing

WARNER BOOKS

A Warner Communications Company

WARNER BOOKS EDITION

Copyright © 1990 by Don "Duck" Edwing, Nick Meglin and
E.C. Publications, Inc.
All rights reserved.
No part of this book may be reproduced without permission.
For information address:
E.C. Publications, Inc.
485 Madison Avenue
New York, N.Y. 10022

Title "MAD" used with permission of its owner,
E.C. Publications, Inc.

This Warner Books Edition is published by
arrangement with E.C. Publications, Inc.

Warner Books, Inc.
666 Fifth Avenue
New York, N.Y. 10103

W A Warner Communications Company

Printed in the United States of America

First Printing: April, 1990

10 9 8 7 6 5 4 3 2 1

ATTENTION SCHOOLS

WARNER books are available at quantity discounts with bulk
purchase for educational use. For information, please write to:
SPECIAL SALES DEPARTMENT, WARNER BOOKS, 666 FIFTH
AVENUE, NEW YORK, NY 10103.

This book is
DUCK-TATED
to my wife
"CLUCK"

D.E.

SO WHO IS THIS MASKED MAN THEY CALL

ZERO

AND WHERE DOES HE COME FROM?
WHO DESIGNS HIS CLOTHES?
AND WHO'S ASKING THESE QUESTIONS?

YOU? WHY BOTHER! ALL YOU HAVE TO
KNOW (AND MAKE SURE YOU DON'T **TELL**
ANYONE--LET THIS BE OUR LITTLE SECRET!)
IS THAT BY *DAY* HE'S ...

... *MARIO*
COHEN,
Fashion Consultant...

AND AT NIGHT HE'S SOMETHING ELSE!
JUST ASK ...
SENORITA CLAIRE,
WHO LOVES ONLY *ONE,*
BUT SINCE THAT ONE
WEARS A *MASK,* SHE'S
DETERMINED TO *TRY*
THEM ALL UNTIL SHE
FINDS *WHICH ONE* IS
ZERO...

...WHICH DOESN'T MAKE HER *FATHER,* THE EVIL *BARON FICARRA,* RULER OF SOUTHERN CAULIFLOWER AND RODEO DRIVE, *TOO HAPPY!* AND SPEAKING OF *FATHERS,* HOW ABOUT...

El Groo, MARIO'S DISAPPOINTED FATHER WHO WANTED A *LINEBACKER* AND NOT A *Fashion Consultant* FOR A *SON...*

...AND *SGT. TORRES?* Huh? WHAT OF *THEM?* LISTEN, THEY'LL HAVE TO TAKE CARE OF THEMSELVES! *WE'VE* GOT OUR *OWN PROBLEMS!*

SO LET'S GET ON WITH OUR *STORY...*

FATHER, MAY I HAVE A WORD WITH YOU?
DON'T INTERRUPT ME WHEN I'M HAVING A FLASHBACK!
POP

...KNOWING THAT IF MA BARKLAY CROSSED THE STREET, IT WAS THE END OF THE **CRIMSON CAT!** BUT HOW TO GET THE OLD BROAD TO TAKE THE FIRST STEP? THE SINISTER MR. SLY HAD A PLAN...

BAIT

GLUE

KLIK!!

BAIT

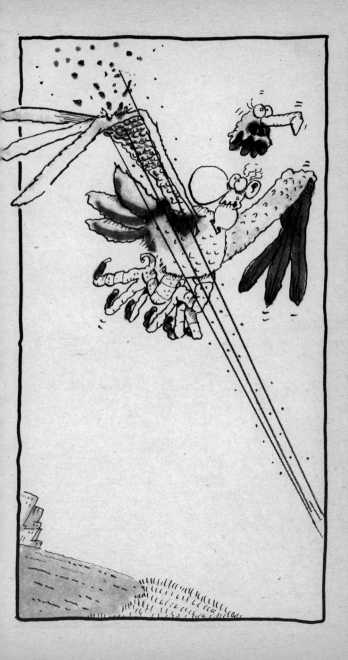

BUZZ WAS *CORRECT* AS USUAL! *STAR WARS* COME AND GO, BUT *TENNIS TITLES* HAVE DEEPER MEANING IN THE *UNIVERSE!* FOR EVEN AS *BUZZ* AND *MEATBALL,* HIS FAMED NAVIGATOR, SPOKE, THE *EVIL* AND *ROTTEN* (*NOT TO MENTION NASTY*) **MONGO** PLOTTED IN HIS *SPACECRAFT* NOT THAT FAR AWAY...

I DON'T KNOW HOW BUZZ ORFF DOES IT, BUT HE MUST HAVE A WEAKNESS!
AND IF HE DOES, I'LL FIND IT! WHAT DOES THE JADED SKULL SAY?
TWENTY PERCENT CHANCE OF RAIN!

...AND THOUGH THE PARTY HAD INDEED STARTED, MOST OF THE CHATTER CENTERED AROUND BATFACE

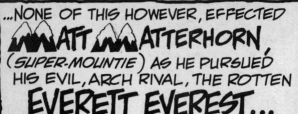

...NONE OF THIS HOWEVER, EFFECTED MATT MATTERHORN, (SUPER-MOUNTIE) AS HE PURSUED HIS EVIL, ARCH RIVAL, THE ROTTEN EVERETT EVEREST...

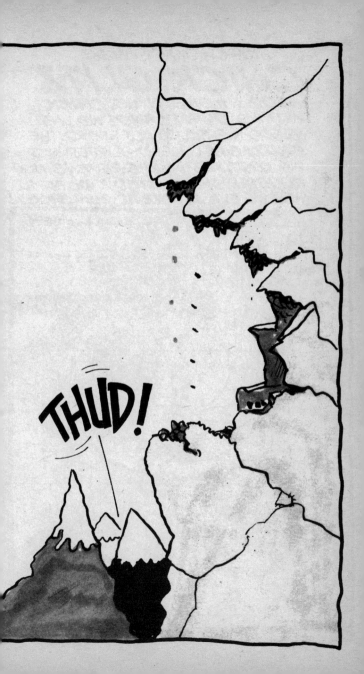

...WHICH DIDN'T PHASE **CHICK GLITZ** FOR A MOMENT! NO, **CHICK** HAD HIS **OWN PLANS!** HIS LAS VEGAS NIGHTCLUB ACT ENDED, THE **SHOW BIZ** LEGEND SLIPPED INTO HIS **COSTUME** AS **THE REVENGING ROOSTER** AND PREPARED TO DO BATTLE WITH THE **EVIL ALPINE AL** -- ON **SKIS!**

BZZZ

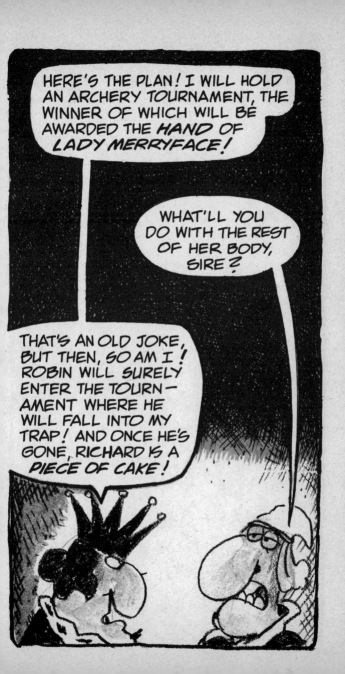

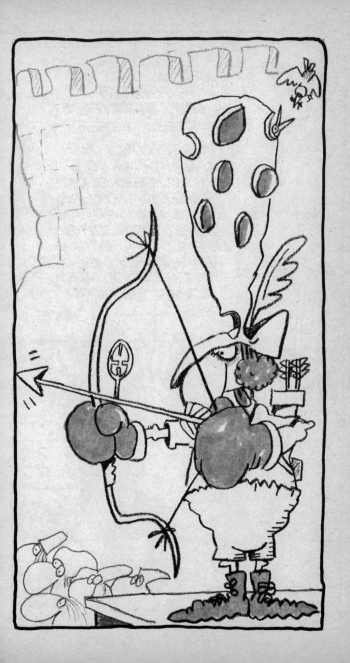

IT MATTERED NOT WHO HAD FREED THE SPOTTED KILLER FROM THE CAGE! WHAT DID MATTER IS HOW TARZANGST, THE FRAUD OF THE JUNGLE, COULD ESCAPE THE SAVAGE BEAST!
ROO WOWR

His **DECEPTIVE PLAY** CAUGHT THE ATTENTION OF COLLEGE **SCOUTS** AND **THE KEP** SOON MOVED ON TO **FAME** AND **GLORY,** (THE TWIN CITIES NORTH OF **DIRE STRAITS** AND SLIGHTLY EAST OF **OBSCURITY**), WHERE HE LED THE **BORO PARK HOOPER-SCOOPERS** TO THEIR FIRST NCBB CHAMPIONSHIP!

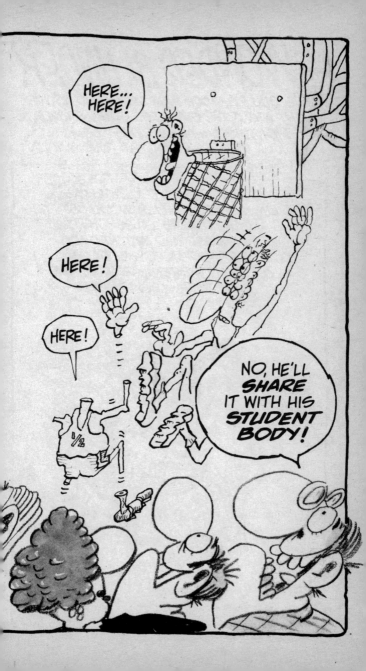

... WHICH STILL LEFT A HOST OF **DOUBTERS** AS TO THE VERY **EXISTENCE** OF **FRUITFLY**...

LET ALONE HIS ABILITY TO **SUCK PLUMS DRY!** LIKE, FOR INSTANCE, THAT **MARCH 18th** AFTERNOON AS HE FLEW AROUND **DOOPO**, A SUBURB OF THE USUALLY PEACEFUL **OJAI, CALIFORNIA**, HOME OF **SERGIO, GROO**, AND OTHER **MARGINALS**...

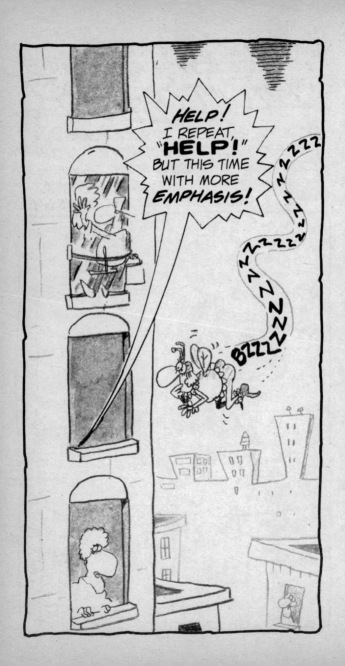

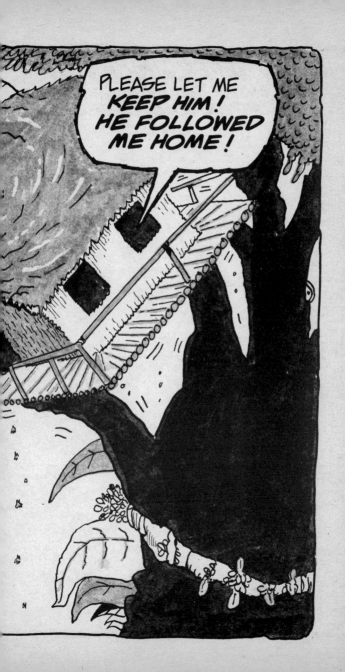

...NOAH NEVERSINK PREPARED TO EVACUATE THE ARMY OF ARK TO THE UPPER REGIONS OF MARIN COUNTY...
FLOOD MODEL
ARK
30 CUBITS HIGH
EASY TO ASSEMBLE
GLUE

THE ADVENTURES OF HEADLOCK HOLMES

From the Diary of DOCTOR WATSNEW

I didn't have to look out into the dark night to know it was foggy and cold, for the eminent criminologist **HEADLOCK HOLMES** was fiddling with his violin as is his wont on foggy, cold evenings. This night in particular, Holmes felt more **MUSIC-ALLY CHALLENGED.** He had removed the **STRINGS** from his instrument and proceeded to play difficult violin pieces by ear, or rather by **NO** ear, since there was **NO SOUND.**

"Watsnew," he said, breaking the silence of his stringless violin playing.

"Nothing much, Holmes, **WHAT'S NEW** with you?" I replied, hoping for some form of acknowledgement for my **HILARIOUS WITTICISM.** But none was forthcoming.

"Watsnew," he repeated, ignoring my humorous attempt completely, "I believe Mozart was in **ERROR** calling for an **A-FLAT** in this section of the concerto. I think an **F-SHARP** is called for. Don't you agree?"

"I'm afraid my ear for **NO-MUSIC** isn't as keen as **YOURS,** my dear Holmes. You could be making countless **mistakes** and I would be the last to know," I chortled.

The master deducer scowled at my audaciousness. I should have **KNOWN BETTER** than to insinuate that Headlock Holmes was capable of making a **MISTAKE** in music or **ANY** other subject in the world.

"Only *JESTING,* my good man," I added quickly, realizing the gravity of my own error. "Just a little joke there."

"*VERY LITTLE,*" he sneered. "I was hoping to discuss profound theories and concepts, but I can see you'd rather employ your questionable wit in silly *WORDPLAY.*"

"Not at all, Holmes," I recanted. "What could be *BETTER* than a chilling fog in the air, my dearest friend filling the room with the *SOUND* of *NO MUSIC,* and endless profound theories and concepts to chew upon? Please Holmes, go on, go on," I said.

But Holmes had already begun, his masterful thoughts drowning out my own inconsequential mumblings, and rightly so, I might add, for as *YOU,* dear reader, may have already *NOTICED,* I do lean a mite in the direction of the *VERBOSE BORE!*

"Take, for example, Watsnew, "*THE CASE OF THE FALLING CONSTABLES!*"

"**BRILLIANT,** Holmes, absolutely **BRILLIANT!**"
"Will you please **SHUT UP,** already? I haven'T
said **ANYTHING BRILLIANT YET,** NOR will I
ever get the opportunity unless you **SHUT**
that perpetual motion **MOUTH** of yours!"
   "I was about to respond, "Brilliant, Holmes,
absolutely brilliant,' for indeed his description
of my verbose ways was **JUST** as he stated,
but I thought better of it."
"Now where was I? Oh, yes,
   "**THE CASE OF THE FALLING
       CONSTABLES...**"

"Hmm, there's **MORE** evil at work in London! Look at this article in The London Fog, Watsnew! "**DEATH BY DROWNING!**"

"There's nothing strange **THERE**, Holmes, I replied. "Many have lost their lives in the **BATH!**"

"This man was in his **BEDROOM**, Watsnew! What do you make of **THAT?**"

"Well, Holmes, I really don't know what to make of it," I replied. "But speaking of **BEDROOMS**, did you hear the one about Tom, the traveling salesman, and the farmer's daughter? It seems..."

"I have no time for your lewd, lascivious tom-foolery! If that last **JACK-THE-SLIPPER** episode didn't tickle your mem-brain, then perhaps..."

"**HAH!** Hold up a minute, Holmes, your rapid-pace wordplay is almost **TOO MUCH** for these rheumy old hands to **NOTATE! 'TOM-FOOLERY! MEM-BRAIN!**' Hah! That's **RICH!**"

"And they let **IDIOTS** like **YOU** beom **DOCTORS**? No **WONDER** we rely on **SOCIALIZED MEDICINE!** Now try and stay with me here as I recall "**THE CASE OF THE DROPLETS OF DEATH...**"

"*Brilliant, Holmes, absolutely brilliant,*" I blurted. "*you're absolutely CORRECT! As usual! A MIND such as yours is indeed a wonder to mankind, womankind, or ANY kind of kind for that matter!*"

But Holmes never heard my lavish praise! His ears were tuned only to the sound of his **STRINGLESS VIOLIN!** He continued to play, sending Mozart's erroneously chosen notes into the cold, foggy night, unheard by **LESSER BEINGS** than he - which, of course, includes us **ALL!**

...WHICH MADE **THE CRIMSON CAT** SNICKER WHEN HE HEARD THE NEWS! NO "*ELECTRIC EYE SYSTEM*" EVER PREVENTED HIM FROM ENTERING A **VAULT** BEFORE, AND THE EVIL **BILL GAINES' VAULT** *OF* **HORROR** WOULD BE NO *EXCEPTION...*

...WHICH HAD NO BEARING ON THE **EVIL, ROTTEN** (NOT TO MENTION **NASTY**) **WARLORD MONGO** WHO WAS STILL FUMING AT THE UNCANNY TURN OF EVENTS! **BUZZ ORFF** HAD WON THE **INTERGALACTIC TENNIS OPEN** (BOTH THE **SINGLES** AND THE **MIXED SINGLES** TITLES), DEFEATING **MONGO'S PROTEGE**, THE ROBOT **LENDL SOUP**...